A Co...
comm...

THE BELGIC CONFESSION

FAITH
ALIVE®
Christian Resources

Grand Rapids, Michigan

Faith Alive Christian Resources published by CRC Publications.
© 1988 CRC Publications, 2850 Kalamazoo SE, Grand Rapids, MI 49560.
All rights reserved. Printed in the United States of America on recycled paper. ✪

Library of Congress Cataloging-in-Publication Data
Christian Reformed Church.
    [Belgic Confession. English]
    A confession of faith commonly known as the Belgic Confession.
      p.   cm.
    "The translation presented here is based on the French text of 1619 and was
adopted by the 1985 Synod of the Christian Reformed Church"—Introd.
    1. Reformed Church–Creeds—Early works to 1800. 2. Christian Reformed
Church—Creeds—Early works to 1800. I. Title.
BX9429.B4C48   1988
238'.42—dc19   88-32157
                                                              CIP

ISBN 0-930265-66-1
10 9 8 7 6

INTRODUCTION

The *Confession of Faith*, popularly known as the *Belgic Confession (Confessio Belgica)*, is one of the oldest doctrinal standards subscribed to by Protestant Christians. First published in Rouen, France, in 1561, the confession was a protest against the Roman Catholic persecution of Protestants in the Netherlands and an attempt to convince the Catholic government of that country that adherents to the Reformed faith were law-abiding citizens who professed the true Christian doctrine according to the Holy Scriptures.

The chief author of this confession, Guido de Brès, was a preacher of the Reformed churches of the Netherlands. In 1562, he and other petitioners sent this confession, with a cover letter, to King Philip II. In the letter these Protestants told Philip that they were ready to obey the government in all lawful things, but that they would "offer their backs to stripes, their tongues to knives, their mouths to gags, and their whole bodies to the fire," rather than deny the truth expressed in this confession.

Although the confession did not immediately gain freedom from persecution for the Protestants, and although de Brès later died for the faith he confessed in this document, the Belgic Confession endured and will continue to endure. In the Netherlands de Brès's work was received gladly by the churches and adopted by national synods held during the last three decades of the sixteenth century. The text, not the contents, was revised again at the Synod of Dort in 1618–19 and adopted as one of the doctrinal standards of Reformed churches. It stands as one of the best symbolical statements of the Reformed doctrine. The translation presented here is based on the French text of 1619 and was adopted by the 1985 Synod of the Christian Reformed Church.

The Belgic Confession

Article 1: *The Only God*

We all believe in our hearts
and confess with our mouths
that there is a single
and simple
spiritual being,
whom we call God—

eternal,
incomprehensible,
invisible,
unchangeable,
infinite,
almighty;

completely wise,
just,
and good,
and the overflowing source
   of all good.

Article 2: *The Means by Which We Know God*

We know him by two means:

First, by the creation, preservation, and government
of the universe,
since that universe is before our eyes
like a beautiful book
  in which all creatures,
  great and small,
  are as letters
  to make us ponder
  the invisible things of God:
    his eternal power
    and his divinity,
    as the apostle Paul says in Romans 1:20.

  All these things are enough to convict men
  and to leave them without excuse.

Second, he makes himself known to us more openly
by his holy and divine Word,
as much as we need in this life,
  for his glory
  and for the salvation of his own.

Article 3: *The Written Word of God*

We confess that this Word of God
was not sent nor delivered by the will of men,
but that holy men of God spoke,
being moved by the Holy Spirit,
  as Peter says.[1]

Afterwards our God—
  because of the special care he has
  for us and our salvation—
commanded his servants,
the prophets and apostles,
to commit this revealed Word to writing.
He himself wrote
with his own finger
the two tables of the law.

Therefore we call such writings
holy and divine Scriptures.

[1] 2 Pet. 1:21

6

Article 4: *The Canonical Books*

We include in the Holy Scripture the two volumes
of the Old and New Testaments.
They are canonical books
with which there can be no quarrel at all.

In the church of God the list is as follows:
In the Old Testament,
    the five books of Moses—
        Genesis, Exodus, Leviticus, Numbers, Deuteronomy;
    the books of Joshua, Judges, and Ruth;
    the two books of Samuel, and two of Kings;
    the two books of Chronicles, called Paralipomenon;
    the first book of Ezra; Nehemiah, Esther, Job;
    the Psalms of David;
    the three books of Solomon—
        Proverbs, Ecclesiastes, and the Song;
    the four major prophets—
        Isaiah, Jeremiah, Ezekiel, Daniel;
    and then the other twelve minor prophets—
        Hosea, Joel, Amos, Obadiah,
        Jonah, Micah, Nahum, Habakkuk,
        Zephaniah, Haggai, Zechariah, Malachi.

In the New Testament,
    the four gospels—
        Matthew, Mark, Luke, and John;
    the Acts of the Apostles;
    the fourteen letters of Paul—
        to the Romans;
        the two letters to the Corinthians;
        to the Galatians, Ephesians, Philippians, and Colossians;
        the two letters to the Thessalonians;
        the two letters to Timothy;
        to Titus, Philemon, and to the Hebrews;
    the seven letters of the other apostles—
        one of James;
        two of Peter;
        three of John;
        one of Jude;
    and the Revelation of the apostle John.

Article 5: *The Authority of Scripture*

We receive all these books
and these only
as holy and canonical,
for the regulating, founding, and establishing
of our faith.

And we believe
without a doubt
all things contained in them—
   not so much because the church
   receives and approves them as such
   but above all because the Holy Spirit
   testifies in our hearts
   that they are from God,
   and also because they
   prove themselves
   to be from God.

   For even the blind themselves are able to see
   that the things predicted in them
   do happen.

Article 6: *The Difference Between Canonical*
and Apocryphal Books

We distinguish between these holy books
and the apocryphal ones,
   which are the third and fourth books of Esdras;
   the books of Tobit, Judith, Wisdom, Jesus Sirach, Baruch;
   what was added to the Story of Esther;
   the Song of the Three Children in the Furnace;
   the Story of Susanna;
   the Story of Bel and the Dragon;
   the Prayer of Manasseh;
   and the two books of Maccabees.

The church may certainly read these books
and learn from them
as far as they agree with the canonical books.
But they do not have such power and virtue
that one could confirm
from their testimony
any point of faith or of the Christian religion.
Much less can they detract
from the authority
of the other holy books.

Article 7: *The Sufficiency of Scripture*

We believe
that this Holy Scripture contains
the will of God completely
and that everything one must believe
to be saved
is sufficiently taught in it.

For since the entire manner of service
which God requires of us
is described in it at great length,
no one—
    even an apostle
    or an angel from heaven,
    as Paul says—[2]
ought to teach other than
what the Holy Scriptures have
already taught us.

For since it is forbidden
to add to or subtract from the Word of God,[3]
this plainly demonstrates
that the teaching is perfect
and complete in all respects.

Therefore we must not consider human writings—
    no matter how holy their authors may have been—
equal to the divine writings;
nor may we put custom,
nor the majority,
nor age,
nor the passage of time or persons,
nor councils, decrees, or official decisions
above the truth of God,
    for truth is above everything else.

For all human beings are liars by nature
and more vain than vanity itself.

Therefore we reject with all our hearts
everything that does not agree
with this infallible rule,
    as we are taught to do by the apostles
    when they say,
        "Test the spirits
        to see if they are of God,"[4]
    and also,

"If anyone comes to you
and does not bring this teaching,
do not receive him
into your house."[5]

[2] Gal. 1:8
[3] Deut. 12:32; Rev. 22:18–19
[4] 1 John 4:1
[5] 2 John 10

Article 8: *The Trinity*

In keeping with this truth and Word of God
we believe in one God,
who is one single essence,
in whom there are three persons,
really, truly, and eternally distinct
according to their incommunicable properties—
    namely,
        Father,
        Son,
        and Holy Spirit.
The Father
    is the cause,
    origin,
    and source of all things,
        visible as well as invisible.

The Son
    is the Word,
    the Wisdom,
    and the image
        of the Father.

The Holy Spirit
    is the eternal power
    and might,
        proceeding from the Father and the Son.

Nevertheless,
this distinction does not divide God into three,
    since Scripture teaches us
    that the Father, the Son, and the Holy Spirit
    each has his own subsistence
    distinguished by characteristics—
    yet in such a way
    that these three persons are
    only one God.

It is evident then
that the Father is not the Son
and that the Son is not the Father,
and that likewise the Holy Spirit is
neither the Father nor the Son.

Nevertheless,
these persons,
thus distinct,
are neither divided
nor fused or mixed together.

For the Father did not take on flesh,
nor did the Spirit,
but only the Son.

The Father was never
without his Son,
nor without his Holy Spirit,
since all these are equal from eternity,
in one and the same essence.

There is neither a first nor a last,
for all three are one
in truth and power,
in goodness and mercy.

Article 9: *The Scriptural Witness on the Trinity*

All these things we know
from the testimonies of Holy Scripture
as well as from the effects of the persons,
especially from those we feel within ourselves.

The testimonies of the Holy Scriptures,
which teach us to believe in this Holy Trinity,
are written in many places of the Old Testament,
which need not be enumerated
but only chosen with discretion.

In the book of Genesis God says,
"Let us make man in our image,
according to our likeness."
So "God created man in his own image"—
indeed, "male and female he created them."[6]
"Behold, man has become like one of us."[7]

It appears from this
that there is a plurality of persons
within the Deity,
    when he says,
    "Let us make man in our image"—
and afterwards he indicates the unity
    when he says,
    "God created."

It is true that he does not say here
how many persons there are—
but what is somewhat obscure to us
in the Old Testament
is very clear in the New.

For when our Lord was baptized in the Jordan,
the voice of the Father was heard saying,
    "This is my dear Son";[8]
the Son was seen in the water;
and the Holy Spirit appeared in the form of a dove.

So, in the baptism of all believers
this form was prescribed by Christ:
    "Baptize all people in the name
    of the Father,
    and of the Son,
    and of the Holy Spirit."[9]

In the Gospel according to Luke
the angel Gabriel says to Mary,
the mother of our Lord:
    "The Holy Spirit will come upon you,
    and the power of the Most High will overshadow you;
    and therefore that holy one to be born of you
    shall be called the Son of God."[10]

And in another place it says:
    "The grace of our Lord Jesus Christ,
    and the love of God,
    and the fellowship of the Holy Spirit
    be with you."[11]

"There are three who bear witness in heaven—
the Father, the Word, and the Holy Spirit—
and these three are one."[12]

In all these passages we are fully taught
that there are three persons
in the one and only divine essence.
And although this doctrine surpasses human understanding,
we nevertheless believe it now,
    through the Word,
waiting to know and enjoy it fully
    in heaven.

Furthermore,
we must note the particular works and activities
of these three persons in relation to us.
    The Father is called our Creator,
        by reason of his power.
    The Son is our Savior and Redeemer,
        by his blood.
    The Holy Spirit is our Sanctifier,
        by his living in our hearts.

This doctrine of the Holy Trinity
has always been maintained in the true church,
    from the time of the apostles until the present,
    against Jews, Muslims,
    and certain false Christians and heretics,
        such as Marcion, Mani,
        Praxeas, Sabellius, Paul of Samosata, Arius,
        and others like them,
        who were rightly condemned by the holy fathers.

And so,
    in this matter we willingly accept
    the three ecumenical creeds—
    the Apostles', Nicene, and Athanasian—
    as well as what the ancient fathers decided
    in agreement with them.

6 Gen. 1:26–27
7 Gen. 3:22
8 Matt. 3:17
9 Matt. 28:19
10 Luke 1:35
11 2 Cor. 13:14
12 1 John 5:7 (KJV)

Article 10: *The Deity of Christ*

We believe that Jesus Christ,
according to his divine nature,
is the only Son of God—
    eternally begotten,
    not made nor created,
        for then he would be a creature.

He is one in essence with the Father;
coeternal;
the exact image of the person of the Father
and the "reflection of his glory,"[13]
    being in all things like him.

He is the Son of God
not only from the time he assumed our nature
but from all eternity,
    as the following testimonies teach us
    when they are taken together.

    Moses says that God "created the world";[14]
    and John says that "all things were created by the Word,"[15]
        which he calls God.
    The apostle says that "God made the world by his Son."[16]
    He also says that "God created all things by Jesus Christ."[17]

And so it must follow
that he who is called God, the Word, the Son, and Jesus Christ
already existed when all things were created by him.
Therefore the prophet Micah says
that his origin is "from ancient times,
    from eternity."[18]
And the apostle says
that he has "neither beginning of days
    nor end of life."[19]

So then,
he is the true eternal God,
the Almighty,
whom we invoke,
worship,
and serve.

[13] Col. 1:15; Heb. 1:3
[14] Gen. 1:1
[15] John 1:3
[16] Heb. 1:2
[17] Col. 1:16
[18] Mic. 5:2
[19] Heb. 7:3

Article 11: *The Deity of the Holy Spirit*

We believe and confess also
that the Holy Spirit proceeds eternally
from the Father and the Son—
    neither made,
    nor created,
    nor begotten,
    but only proceeding
    from the two of them.

In regard to order,
he is the third person of the Trinity—
    of one and the same essence,
    and majesty,
    and glory,
    with the Father and the Son.

He is true and eternal God,
    as the Holy Scriptures teach us.

Article 12: *The Creation of All Things*

We believe that the Father
created heaven and earth and all other creatures
from nothing,
when it seemed good to him,
by his Word—
    that is to say,
    by his Son.

He has given all creatures
their being, form, and appearance,
and their various functions
    for serving their Creator.

Even now
he also sustains and governs them all,
according to his eternal providence,
and by his infinite power,
    that they may serve man,
    in order that man may serve God.

He has also created the angels good,
that they might be his messengers
and serve his elect.

Some of them have fallen
    from the excellence in which God created them
    into eternal perdition;
and the others have persisted and remained
    in their orginal state,
    by the grace of God.

The devils and evil spirits are so corrupt
that they are enemies of God
and of everything good.
They lie in wait for the church
and every member of it
like thieves,
    with all their power,
to destroy and spoil everything
    by their deceptions.

So then,
by their own wickedness
they are condemned to everlasting damnation,
    daily awaiting their torments.

For that reason
we detest the error of the Sadducees,
    who deny that there are spirits and angels,
and also the error of the Manicheans,
    who say that the devils originated by themselves,
    being evil by nature,
        without having been corrupted.

Article 13: *The Doctrine of God's Providence*

We believe that this good God,
    after he created all things,
did not abandon them to chance or fortune
but leads and governs them
    according to his holy will,
in such a way that nothing happens in this world
without his orderly arrangement.

Yet God is not the author of,
nor can he be charged with,
the sin that occurs.
For his power and goodness
are so great and incomprehensible
that he arranges and does his work very well and justly
even when the devils and wicked men act unjustly.

We do not wish to inquire
  with undue curiosity
into what he does that surpasses human understanding
  and is beyond our ability to comprehend.
But in all humility and reverence
we adore the just judgments of God,
which are hidden from us,
    being content to be Christ's disciples,
      so as to learn only what he shows us in his Word,
        without going beyond those limits.

This doctrine gives us unspeakable comfort
since it teaches us
that nothing can happen to us by chance
but only by the arrangement of our gracious
heavenly Father.
He watches over us with fatherly care,
keeping all creatures under his control,
so that not one of the hairs on our heads
(for they are all numbered)
nor even a little bird
can fall to the ground
without the will of our Father.[20]

In this thought we rest,
knowing that he holds in check
the devils and all our enemies,
    who cannot hurt us
    without his permission and will.

For that reason we reject
the damnable error of the Epicureans,
    who say that God involves himself in nothing
    and leaves everything to chance.

[20] Matt. 10:29–30

Article 14: *The Creation and Fall of Man*

We believe
that God created man from the dust of the earth
and made and formed him in his image and likeness—
    good, just, and holy;
    able by his own will to conform
    in all things
    to the will of God.

But when he was in honor
he did not understand it[21]
and did not recognize his excellence.
But he subjected himself willingly to sin
and consequently to death and the curse,
    lending his ear to the word of the devil.

For he transgressed the commandment of life,
    which he had received,
and by his sin he separated himself from God,
    who was his true life,
having corrupted his entire nature.

So he made himself guilty
and subject to physical and spiritual death,
    having become wicked,
    perverse,
    and corrupt in all his ways.
He lost all his excellent gifts
    which he had received from God,
and he retained none of them
except for small traces
    which are enough to make him
    inexcusable.

Moreover, all the light in us is turned to darkness,
as the Scripture teaches us:
    "The light shone in the darkness,
    and the darkness did not receive it."[22]
Here John calls men "darkness."

Therefore we reject everything taught to the contrary
concerning man's free will,
since man is nothing but the slave of sin
and cannot do a thing
unless it is "given him from heaven."[23]

For who can boast of being able
to do anything good by himself,
since Christ says,

> "No one can come to me
> unless my Father who sent me
> draws him"?[24]

Who can glory in his own will
> when he understands that "the mind of the flesh
> is enmity against God"?[25]

Who can speak of his own knowledge
> in view of the fact that "the natural man
> does not understand the things of the Spirit of God"?[26]

In short,
who can produce a single thought,
> since he knows that we are "not able to think a thing"
> about ourselves,
> by ourselves,
> but that "our ability is from God"?[27]

And therefore,
what the apostle says
ought rightly to stand fixed and firm:
> "God works within us both to will and to do
> according to his good pleasure."[28]

For there is no understanding nor will
conforming to God's understanding and will
apart from Christ's involvement,
> as he teaches us when he says,
> "Without me you can do nothing."[29]

[21] Ps. 49:20
[22] John 1:5
[23] John 3:27
[24] John 6:44
[25] Rom. 8:7
[26] 1 Cor. 2:14
[27] 2 Cor. 3:5
[28] Phil. 2:13
[29] John 15:5

Article 15: *The Doctrine of Original Sin*

We believe
that by the disobedience of Adam
original sin has been spread
through the whole human race.

It is a corruption of all nature—
an inherited depravity which even infects small infants
    in their mother's womb,
and the root which produces in man
    every sort of sin.
It is therefore so vile and enormous in God's sight
that it is enough to condemn the human race,
and it is not abolished
    or wholly uprooted
    even by baptism,
        seeing that sin constantly boils forth
        as though from a contaminated spring.

Nevertheless,
it is not imputed to God's children
for their condemnation
but is forgiven
by his grace and mercy—
    not to put them to sleep
    but so that the awareness of this corruption
    might often make believers groan
    as they long to be set free
    from the "body of this death."[30]

Therefore we reject the error of the Pelagians
who say that this sin is nothing else than a matter of
imitation.

[30] Rom. 7:24

Article 16: *The Doctrine of Election*

We believe that—
   all Adam's descendants having thus fallen
   into perdition and ruin
   by the sin of the first man—
God showed himself to be as he is:
merciful and just.

He is merciful
in withdrawing and saving from this perdition those whom he,
   in his eternal and unchangeable counsel,
has elected and chosen in Jesus Christ our Lord
   by his pure goodness,
   without any consideration of their works.

He is just
in leaving the others in their ruin and fall
   into which they plunged themselves.

Article 17: *The Recovery of Fallen Man*

We believe that our good God,
by his marvelous wisdom and goodness,
   seeing that man had plunged himself in this manner
   into both physical and spiritual death
   and made himself completely miserable,
set out to find him,
though man,
   trembling all over,
was fleeing from him.

And he comforted him,
promising to give him his Son,
   "born of a woman,"[31]
to crush the head of the serpent,[32]
and to make him blessed.

[31] Gal. 4:4
[32] Gen. 3:15

Article 18: *The Incarnation*

So then we confess
that God fulfilled the promise
   which he had made to the early fathers
   by the mouth of his holy prophets
when he sent his only and eternal Son
into the world
at the time set by him.

The Son took the "form of a servant"
and was made in the "likeness of man,"[33]
   truly assuming a real human nature,
   with all its weaknesses,
   except for sin;
   being conceived in the womb of the blessed virgin Mary
   by the power of the Holy Spirit,
   without male participation.

And he not only assumed human nature
   as far as the body is concerned
but also a real human soul,
   in order that he might be a real human being.
For since the soul had been lost as well as the body
he had to assume them both
to save them both together.

Therefore we confess,
   against the heresy of the Anabaptists
   who deny that Christ assumed human flesh
     from his mother,
that he "shared the very flesh and blood of children";[34]
that he is "fruit of the loins of David" according to the flesh;[35]
"born of the seed of David" according to the flesh;[36]
"fruit of the womb of the virgin Mary";[37]
"born of a woman";[38]
"the seed of David";[39]
"a shoot from the root of Jesse";[40]
"the offspring of Judah,"[41]
   having descended from the Jews according to the flesh;
"from the seed of Abraham"—
   for he "assumed Abraham's seed"
   and was "made like his brothers
     except for sin."[42]

In this way he is truly our Immanuel—
   that is: "God with us."[43]

[33] Phil. 2:7
[34] Heb. 2:14
[35] Acts 2:30
[36] Rom. 1:3
[37] Luke 1:42
[38] Gal. 4:4
[39] 2 Tim. 2:8
[40] Rom. 15:12
[41] Heb. 7:14
[42] Heb. 2:17; 4:15
[43] Matt. 1:23

Article 19: *The Two Natures of Christ*

We believe that by being thus conceived
the person of the Son has been inseparably united
and joined together
with human nature,
    in such a way that there are not two Sons of God,
    nor two persons,
    but two natures united in a single person,
    with each nature retaining its own distinct properties.

Thus his divine nature has always remained uncreated,
    without beginning of days or end of life,[44]
    filling heaven and earth.

His human nature has not lost its properties
but continues to have those of a creature—
    it has a beginning of days;
    it is of a finite nature
    and retains all that belongs to a real body.
    And even though he,
    by his resurrection,
    gave it immortality,
    that nonetheless did not change
    the reality of his human nature;
    for our salvation and resurrection
    depend also on the reality of his body.

But these two natures
are so united together in one person
that they are not even separated by his death.

So then,
what he committed to his Father when he died
was a real human spirit which left his body.
But meanwhile his divine nature remained
united with his human nature
    even when he was lying in the grave;
and his deity never ceased to be in him,
    just as it was in him when he was a little child,
    though for a while it did not show itself as such.

These are the reasons why we confess him
to be true God and true man—
    true God in order to conquer death
      by his power,
    and true man that he might die for us
      in the weakness of his flesh.

[44] Heb. 7:3

Article 20: *The Justice and Mercy of God in Christ*

We believe that God—
  who is perfectly merciful
  and also very just—
sent his Son to assume the nature
in which the disobedience had been committed,
  in order to bear in it the punishment of sin
  by his most bitter passion and death.

So God made known his justice toward his Son,
  who was charged with our sin,
and he poured out his goodness and mercy on us,
  who are guilty and worthy of damnation,
giving to us his Son to die,
  by a most perfect love,
and raising him to life
  for our justification,
    in order that by him
    we might have immortality
    and eternal life.

Article 21: *The Atonement*

We believe
that Jesus Christ is a high priest forever
according to the order of Melchizedek—
  made such by an oath—
and that he presented himself
in our name
before his Father,
to appease his wrath
with full satisfaction
  by offering himself
    on the tree of the cross
  and pouring out his precious blood
    for the cleansing of our sins,
    as the prophets had predicted.

For it is written
that "the chastisement of our peace"
was placed on the Son of God
and that "we are healed by his wounds."
He was "led to death as a lamb";
he was "numbered among sinners"[45]
and condemned as a criminal by Pontius Pilate,
  though Pilate had declared
  that he was innocent.

So he paid back
what he had not stolen,[46]
and he suffered—
    the "just for the unjust,"[47]
    in both his body and his soul—
in such a way that
when he sensed the horrible punishment
required by our sins
his sweat became like "big drops of blood
falling on the ground."[48]
He cried, "My God, my God,
why have you abandoned me?"[49]

And he endured all this
for the forgiveness of our sins.

Therefore we rightly say with Paul that
we "know nothing but Jesus and him crucified";[50]
we consider all things as "dung
for the excellence of the knowledge
of our Lord Jesus Christ."[51]
We find all comforts in his wounds
and have no need to seek or invent any other means
to reconcile ourselves with God
than this one and only sacrifice,
once made,
which renders believers perfect
forever.

This is also why
the angel of God called him Jesus—
that is, "Savior"—
    because he would save his people
    from their sins.[52]

[45] Isa. 53:4–12
[46] Ps. 69:4
[47] 1 Pet. 3:18
[48] Luke 22:44
[49] Matt. 27:46
[50] 1 Cor. 2:2
[51] Phil. 3:8
[52] Matt. 1:21

Article 22: *The Righteousness of Faith*

We believe that
for us to acquire the true knowledge of this great mystery
the Holy Spirit kindles in our hearts a true faith
that embraces Jesus Christ,
    with all his merits,
and makes him its own,
and no longer looks for anything
    apart from him.

For it must necessarily follow
that either all that is required for our salvation
is not in Christ or,
if all is in him,
then he who has Christ by faith
has his salvation entirely.

Therefore,
to say that Christ is not enough
but that something else is needed as well
is a most enormous blasphemy against God—
    for it then would follow
    that Jesus Christ is only half a Savior.
And therefore we justly say with Paul
that we are justified "by faith alone"
or by faith "apart from works."[53]

However,
we do not mean,
properly speaking,
that it is faith itself that justifies us—
    for faith is only the instrument
    by which we embrace Christ,
    our righteousness.

But Jesus Christ is our righteousness
    in making available to us all his merits
    and all the holy works he has done
    for us and in our place.
And faith is the instrument
    that keeps us in communion with him
    and with all his benefits.

When those benefits are made ours
they are more than enough to absolve us
of our sins.

[53] Rom. 3:28

Article 23: *The Justification of Sinners*

We believe
that our blessedness lies in the forgiveness of our sins
because of Jesus Christ,
and that in it our righteousness before God is contained,
    as David and Paul teach us
    when they declare that man blessed
    to whom God grants righteousness
    apart from works.[54]

And the same apostle says
that we are justified "freely" or "by grace"
through redemption in Jesus Christ.[55]
And therefore we cling to this foundation,
which is firm forever,
    giving all glory to God,
    humbling ourselves,
    and recognizing ourselves as we are;
    not claiming a thing for ourselves or our merits
    and leaning and resting
        on the sole obedience of Christ crucified,
            which is ours when we believe in him.

That is enough to cover all our sins
and to make us confident,
freeing the conscience from the fear, dread, and terror
    of God's approach,
without doing what our first father, Adam, did,
    who trembled as he tried to cover himself
        with fig leaves.

In fact,
if we had to appear before God relying—
    no matter how little—
on ourselves or some other creature,
then, alas, we would be swallowed up.

Therefore everyone must say with David:
"Lord, do not enter into judgment with your servants,
    for before you no living person shall be justified."[56]

[54] Ps. 32:1; Rom. 4:6
[55] Rom. 3:24
[56] Ps. 143:2

Article 24: *The Sanctification of Sinners*

We believe that this true faith,
    produced in man by the hearing of God's Word
    and by the work of the Holy Spirit,
regenerates him and makes him a "new man,"[57]
    causing him to live the "new life"[58]
    and freeing him from the slavery of sin.

Therefore,
far from making people cold
toward living in a pious and holy way,
this justifying faith,
quite to the contrary,
so works within them that
    apart from it
they will never do a thing out of love for God
but only out of love for themselves
and fear of being condemned.

So then, it is impossible
for this holy faith to be unfruitful in a human being,
seeing that we do not speak of an empty faith
but of what Scripture calls
"faith working through love,"[59]
    which leads a man to do by himself
    the works that God has commanded
      in his Word.

These works,
    proceeding from the good root of faith,
are good and acceptable to God,
    since they are all sanctified by his grace.
Yet they do not count toward our justification—
    for by faith in Christ we are justified,
    even before we do good works.
      Otherwise they could not be good,
      any more than the fruit of a tree could be good
      if the tree is not good in the first place.

So then, we do good works,
but not for merit—
    for what would we merit?
Rather, we are indebted to God for the good works we do,
    and not he to us,
since it is he who "works in us both to will and do
    according to his good pleasure"[60]—
thus keeping in mind what is written:
    "When you have done all that is commanded you,
    then you shall say, 'We are unworthy servants;
    we have done what it was our duty to do.' "[61]

Yet we do not wish to deny
that God rewards good works—
but it is by his grace
that he crowns his gifts.

Moreover,
although we do good works
we do not base our salvation on them;
    for we cannot do any work
    that is not defiled by our flesh
    and also worthy of punishment.
And even if we could point to one,
    memory of a single sin is enough
    for God to reject that work.

So we would always be in doubt,
    tossed back and forth
    without any certainty,
and our poor consciences would be tormented constantly
    if they did not rest on the merit
    of the suffering and death of our Savior.

[57] 2 Cor. 5:17
[58] Rom. 6:4
[59] Gal. 5:6
[60] Phil. 2:13
[61] Luke 17:10

Article 25: *The Fulfillment of the Law*

We believe
that the ceremonies and symbols of the law have ended
   with the coming of Christ,
and that all foreshadowings have come to an end,
so that the use of them ought to be abolished
   among Christians.
Yet the truth and substance of these things
remain for us in Jesus Christ,
   in whom they have been fulfilled.

Nevertheless,
we continue to use the witnesses
drawn from the law and prophets
   to confirm us in the gospel
   and to regulate our lives with full integrity
      for the glory of God,
      according to his will.

Article 26: *The Intercession of Christ*

We believe that we have no access to God
except through the one and only Mediator and Intercessor:
Jesus Christ the Righteous.[62]

He therefore was made man,
uniting together the divine and human natures,
so that we human beings might have access to the divine Majesty.
Otherwise we would have no access.

But this Mediator,
   whom the Father has appointed between himself and us,
ought not terrify us by his greatness,
   so that we have to look for another one,
   according to our fancy.
For neither in heaven nor among the creatures on earth
is there anyone who loves us
more than Jesus Christ does.
   Although he was "in the form of God,"
   he nevertheless "emptied himself,"
   taking the form of "a man" and "a servant" for us;[63]
   and he made himself "completely like his brothers."[64]

Suppose we had to find another intercessor.
Who would love us more than he who gave his life for us,
even though "we were his enemies"?[65]
And suppose we had to find one who has prestige and power.
Who has as much of these as he who is seated
"at the right hand of the Father,"[66]
and who has all power
"in heaven and on earth"?[67]
And who will be heard more readily
than God's own dearly beloved Son?

So then, sheer unbelief has led to the practice
of dishonoring the saints,
instead of honoring them.
That was something the saints never did nor asked for,
but which in keeping with their duty,
as appears from their writings,
they consistently refused.

We should not plead here
that we are unworthy—
for it is not a question of offering our prayers
on the basis of our own dignity
but only on the basis of the excellence and dignity
of Jesus Christ,
whose righteousness is ours
by faith.

Since the apostle for good reason
wants us to get rid of this foolish fear—
or rather, this unbelief—
he says to us that Jesus Christ
was "made like his brothers in all things,"
that he might be a high priest
who is merciful and faithful
to purify the sins of the people.[68]
For since he suffered,
being tempted,
he is also able to help those
who are tempted.[69]

And further,
to encourage us more
to approach him
he says,
"Since we have a high priest,
Jesus the Son of God,
who has entered into heaven,
we maintain our confession.
For we do not have a high priest
who is unable to have compassion for our weaknesses,
but one who was tempted in all things,
just as we are,
except for sin.
Let us go then
with confidence
to the throne of grace
that we may obtain mercy
and find grace,
in order to be helped."[70]

The same apostle says that
we "have liberty to enter into the Holy Place
by the blood of Jesus.
Let us go, then, in the assurance
of faith. . . ."[71]

Likewise
"Christ's priesthood is forever.
By this he is able to save completely
those who draw near to God through him
who always lives to intercede
for them."[72]

What more do we need?
For Christ himself declares:
"I am the way, the truth, and the life;
no one comes to my Father
but by me."[73]
Why should we seek
another intercessor?

Since it has pleased God
to give us his Son as our Intercessor,
let us not leave him for another—
    or rather seek, without ever finding.
For when God gave him to us
he knew well that we were sinners.

Therefore,
in following the command of Christ
we call on the heavenly Father
through Christ,
our only Mediator,
as we are taught by the Lord's Prayer,
   being assured that we shall obtain
   all we ask of the Father
   in his name.

[62] 1 John 2:1
[63] Phil. 2:6–8
[64] Heb. 2:17
[65] Rom. 5:10
[66] Rom. 8:34; Heb. 1:3
[67] Matt. 28:18
[68] Heb. 2:17
[69] Heb. 2:18
[70] Heb. 4:14–16
[71] Heb. 10:19, 22
[72] Heb. 7:24–25
[73] John 14:6

Article 27: *The Holy Catholic Church*

We believe and confess
one single catholic or universal church—
   a holy congregation and gathering
   of true Christian believers,
      awaiting their entire salvation in Jesus Christ
      being washed by his blood,
      and sanctified and sealed by the Holy Spirit.

This church has existed from the beginning of the world
and will last until the end,
   as appears from the fact
   that Christ is eternal King
   who cannot be without subjects.

And this holy church is preserved by God
against the rage of the whole world,
   even though for a time
   it may appear very small
   in the eyes of men—
   as though it were snuffed out.

For example,
during the very dangerous time of Ahab
the Lord preserved for himself seven thousand men
who did not bend their knees to Baal.[74]

And so this holy church
is not confined,
bound,
or limited to a certain place or certain persons.
But it is spread and dispersed
throughout the entire world,
  though still joined and united
    in heart and will,
    in one and the same Spirit,
    by the power of faith.

[74] 1 Kings 19:18

Article 28: *The Obligations of Church Members*

We believe that
  since this holy assembly and congregation
  is the gathering of those who are saved
  and there is no salvation apart from it,
no one ought to withdraw from it,
  content to be by himself,
  regardless of his status or condition.

But all people are obliged
to join and unite with it,
keeping the unity of the church
  by submitting to its instruction and discipline,
  by bending their necks under the yoke of Jesus Christ,
  and by serving to build up one another,
according to the gifts God has given them
as members of each other
in the same body.

And to preserve this unity more effectively,
it is the duty of all believers,
  according to God's Word,
to separate themselves
from those who do not belong to the church,
  in order to join this assembly
  wherever God has established it,
    even if civil authorities and royal decrees forbid
    and death and physical punishment result.

And so,
all who withdraw from the church
or do not join it
act contrary to God's ordinance.

Article 29: *The Marks of the True Church*

We believe that we ought to discern
  diligently and very carefully,
  by the Word of God,
what is the true church—
  for all sects in the world today
  claim for themselves the name of "the church."

We are not speaking here of the company of hypocrites
who are mixed among the good in the church
and who nonetheless are not part of it,
even though they are physically there.
But we are speaking of distinguishing
the body and fellowship of the true church
from all sects that call themselves "the church."

The true church can be recognized
if it has the following marks:
  The church engages in the pure preaching
    of the gospel;
  it makes use of the pure administration of the sacraments
    as Christ instituted them;
  it practices church discipline
    for correcting faults.
In short, it governs itself
according to the pure Word of God,
  rejecting all things contrary to it
  and holding Jesus Christ as the only Head.
By these marks one can be assured
of recognizing the true church—
  and no one ought to be separated from it.

As for those who can belong to the church,
we can recognize them by the distinguishing marks of Christians:
  namely by faith,
  and by their fleeing from sin and pursuing righteousness,
    once they have received the one and only Savior,
    Jesus Christ.
They love the true God and their neighbors,
  without turning to the right or left,
and they crucify the flesh and its works.

Though great weakness remains in them,
they fight against it
by the Spirit
all the days of their lives,
appealing constantly

to the blood, suffering, death, and obedience of the Lord Jesus,
   in whom they have forgiveness of their sins,
   through faith in him.

As for the false church,
it assigns more authority to itself and its ordinances
   than to the Word of God;
it does not want to subject itself
   to the yoke of Christ;
it does not administer the sacraments
   as Christ commanded in his Word;
it rather adds to them or subtracts from them
   as it pleases;
it bases itself on men,
   more than on Jesus Christ;
it persecutes those
   who live holy lives according to the Word of God
   and who rebuke it for its faults, greed, and idolatry.

These two churches
are easy to recognize
and thus to distinguish
from each other.

Article 30: *The Government of the Church*

We believe that this true church
ought to be governed according to the spiritual order
that our Lord has taught us in his Word.
   There should be ministers or pastors
      to preach the Word of God
      and adminster the sacraments.
   There should also be elders and deacons,
      along with the pastors,
      to make up the council of the church.

By this means
true religion is preserved;
true doctrine is able to take its course;
and evil men are corrected spiritually and held in check,
   so that also the poor
   and all the afflicted
   may be helped and comforted
   according to their need.

By this means
everything will be done well
and in good order

in the church,
    when such persons are elected
    who are faithful
    and are chosen according to the rule
    that Paul gave to Timothy.[75]

[75] 1 Tim. 3

Article 31: *The Officers of the Church*

We believe that
ministers of the Word of God, elders, and deacons
ought to be chosen to their offices
by a legitimate election of the church,
with prayer in the name of the Lord,
and in good order,
    as the Word of God teaches.

So everyone must be careful
not to push one's self forward improperly,
but all must wait until called by God,
    so that they may be assured of their calling
    and be certain and sure that it is
    from the Lord.

As for the ministers of the Word,
they all have the same power and authority,
    no matter where they may be,
since they are all servants of Jesus Christ,
    the only universal bishop,
    and the only head of the church.

Moreover,
to keep God's holy order
from being violated or despised,
we say that everyone ought,
as much as possible,
to hold the ministers of the Word and elders of the church
in special esteem,
    because of the work they do,
and be at peace with them,
    without grumbling, quarreling, or fighting.

Article 32: *The Order and Discipline of the Church*

We also believe that
although it is useful and good
for those who govern the churches

to establish and set up
a certain order among themselves
for maintaining the body of the church,
they ought always to guard against deviating
from what Christ,
our only Master,
has ordained
for us.

Therefore we reject all human innovations
and all laws imposed on us,
in our worship of God,
which bind and force our consciences
in any way.

So we accept only what is proper
to maintain harmony and unity
and to keep all in obedience
to God.

To that end excommunication,
with all it involves,
according to the Word of God,
is required.

Article 33: *The Sacraments*

We believe that our good God,
mindful of our crudeness and weakness,
has ordained sacraments for us,
  to seal his promises in us,
    to pledge his good will and grace toward us,
    and also to nourish and sustain our faith.

He has added these to the Word of the gospel
to represent better to our external senses
both what he enables us to understand by his Word
and what he does inwardly in our hearts,
  confirming in us
  the salvation he imparts to us.

For they are visible signs and seals
of something internal and invisible,
  by means of which God works in us
  through the power of the Holy Spirit.
So they are not empty and hollow signs
to fool and deceive us,
  for their truth is Jesus Christ,
  without whom they would be nothing.

Moreover,
we are satisfied with the number of sacraments
that Christ our Master has ordained for us.
There are only two:
   the sacrament of baptism
   and the Holy Supper of Jesus Christ.

Article 34: *The Sacrament of Baptism*

We believe and confess that Jesus Christ,
in whom the law is fulfilled,
has by his shed blood
put an end to every other shedding of blood,
   which anyone might do or wish to do
   in order to atone or satisfy for sins.

Having abolished circumcision,
which was done with blood,
he established in its place
the sacrament of baptism.
   By it we are received into God's church
   and set apart from all other people and alien religions,
   that we may be dedicated entirely to him,
      bearing his mark and sign.
   It also witnesses to us
   that he will be our God forever,
      since he is our gracious Father.

Therefore he has commanded
that all those who belong to him
be baptized with pure water
   "in the name of the Father,
   and of the Son,
   and of the Holy Spirit."[76]

In this way he signifies to us
that just as water washes away the dirt of the body
when it is poured on us
and also is seen on the body of the baptized
when it is sprinkled on him,
so too the blood of Christ does the same thing internally,
in the soul,
by the Holy Spirit.
   It washes and cleanses it from its sins
   and transforms us from being the children of wrath
   into the children of God.

This does not happen by the physical water
but by the sprinkling of the precious blood of the Son of God,
who is our Red Sea,
through which we must pass
    to escape the tyranny of Pharoah,
        who is the devil,
    and to enter the spiritual land
        of Canaan.

So ministers,
as far as their work is concerned,
give us the sacrament and what is visible,
but our Lord gives what the sacrament signifies—
namely the invisible gifts and graces;
    washing, purifying, and cleansing our souls
        of all filth and unrighteousness;
    renewing our hearts and filling them
        with all comfort;
    giving us true assurance
        of his fatherly goodness;
    clothing us with the "new man" and stripping off the "old,"
        with all its works.

For this reason we believe that
anyone who aspires to reach eternal life
ought to be baptized only once
without ever repeating it—
for we cannot be born twice.
Yet this baptism is profitable
not only when the water is on us
and when we receive it
but throughout our
entire lives.

For that reason we detest the error of the Anabaptists
    who are not content with a single baptism
        once received
    and also condemn the baptism
        of the children of believers.
    We believe our children ought to be baptized
    and sealed with the sign of the covenant,
        as little children were circumcised in Israel
        on the basis of the same promises
        made to our children.

And truly,
Christ has shed his blood no less
for washing the little children of believers
than he did for adults.

Therefore they ought to receive the sign and sacrament
of what Christ has done for them,
    just as the Lord commanded in the law that
    by offering a lamb for them
    the sacrament of the suffering and death of Christ
    would be granted them
    shortly after their birth.
    This was the sacrament of Jesus Christ.

Furthermore,
baptism does for our children
what circumcision did for the Jewish people.
That is why Paul calls baptism
the "circumcision of Christ."[77]

[76] Matt. 28:19
[77] Col. 2:11

Article 35: *The Sacrament of the Lord's Supper*

We believe and confess
that our Savior Jesus Christ
has ordained and instituted the sacrament of the Holy Supper
to nourish and sustain those
who are already born again and ingrafted
into his family:
his church.

Now those who are born again have two lives in them.
The one is physical and temporal—
    they have it from the moment of their first birth,
    and it is common to all.
The other is spiritual and heavenly,
    and is given them in their second birth;
    it comes through the Word of the gospel
    in the communion of the body of Christ;
    and this life is common to God's elect only.

Thus, to support the physical and earthly life
God has prescribed for us
an appropriate earthly and material bread,
which is as common to all
as life itself also is.
But to maintain the spiritual and heavenly life
that belongs to believers
he has sent a living bread
that came down from heaven:
namely Jesus Christ,
    who nourishes and maintains

41

the spiritual life of believers
when eaten—
that is, when appropriated
and received spiritually
by faith.

To represent to us
this spiritual and heavenly bread
Christ has instituted
an earthly and visible bread as the sacrament of his body
and wine as the sacrament of his blood.
He did this to testify to us that
just as truly as we take and hold the sacraments in our hands
and eat and drink it in our mouths,
    by which our life is then sustained,
so truly we receive into our souls,
    for our spiritual life,
the true body and true blood of Christ,
    our only Savior.
We receive these by faith,
    which is the hand and mouth of our souls.

Now it is certain
that Jesus Christ did not prescribe
his sacraments for us in vain,
since he works in us all he represents
by these holy signs,
    although the manner in which he does it
    goes beyond our understanding
    and is incomprehensible to us,
        just as the operation of God's Spirit
        is hidden and incomprehensible.

Yet we do not go wrong when we say
that what is eaten is Christ's own natural body
and what is drunk is his own blood—
but the manner in which we eat it
is not by the mouth but by the Spirit,
through faith.

In that way Jesus Christ remains always seated
at the right hand of God his Father
in heaven—
but he never refrains on that account
to communicate himself to us
through faith.

This banquet is a spiritual table
at which Christ communicates himself to us
with all his benefits.
At that table he makes us enjoy himself
as much as the merits of his suffering and death,
as he nourishes, strengthens, and comforts
our poor, desolate souls
    by the eating of his flesh,
and relieves and renews them
    by the drinking of his blood.

Moreover,
though the sacraments and thing signified are joined together,
not all receive both of them.
The wicked person certainly takes the sacrament,
to his condemnation,
but does not receive the truth of the sacrament,
    just as Judas and Simon the Sorcerer both indeed
    received the sacrament,
    but not Christ,
    who was signified by it.
    He is communicated only to believers.

Finally,
with humility and reverence
we receive the holy sacrament
in the gathering of God's people,
    as we engage together,
    with thanksgiving,
    in a holy remembrance
    of the death of Christ our Savior,
    and as we thus confess
    our faith and Christian religion.
Therefore no one should come to this table
without examining himself carefully,
    lest "by eating this bread
    and drinking this cup
    he eat and drink to his own judgment."[78]

In short,
by the use of this holy sacrament
we are moved to a fervent love
of God and our neighbors.

Therefore we reject
as desecrations of the sacraments
all the muddled ideas and damnable inventions
that men have added and mixed in with them.

And we say that we should be content with the procedure
that Christ and the apostles have taught us
and speak of these things
as they have spoken of them.

[78] 1 Cor. 11:27

Article 36: *The Civil Government*

We believe that
because of the depravity of the human race
our good God has ordained kings, princes, and civil officers.
He wants the world to be governed by laws and policies
so that human lawlessness may be restrained
and that everything may be conducted in good order
among human beings.

For that purpose he has placed the sword
in the hands of the government,
to punish evil people
and protect the good.

And being called in this manner
to contribute to the advancement of a society
that is pleasing to God,
the civil rulers have the task,
    subject to God's law,
of removing every obstacle
    to the preaching of the gospel
    and to every aspect of divine worship.

They should do this
while completely refraining from every tendency
    toward exercising absolute authority,
and while functioning in the sphere entrusted to them,
    with the means belonging to them.

They should do it in order that
    the Word of God may have free course;
    the kingdom of Jesus Christ may make progress;
    and every anti-Christian power may be resisted.*

---

*The Synod of 1958, in line with 1910 and 1938, substituted the above statement for the following (which it
judged unbiblical): And the government's task is not limited
to caring for and watching over the public domain
but extends also to upholding the sacred ministry,
    with a view to removing and destroying
        all idolatry and false worship of the Antichrist;
    to promoting the kingdom of Jesus Christ;
    and to furthering the preaching of the gospel everywhere;
    to the end that God may be honored and served by everyone,
    as he requires in his Word.

Moreover everyone,
regardless of status, condition, or rank,
must be subject to the government,
and pay taxes,
and hold its representatives in honor and respect,
and obey them in all things that are not in conflict
    with God's Word,
praying for them
    that the Lord may be willing to lead them
        in all their ways
    and that we may live a peaceful and quiet life
        in all piety and decency.*

Article 37: *The Last Judgment*

Finally we believe,
according to God's Word,
that when the time appointed by the Lord is come
(which is unknown to all creatures)
and the number of the elect is complete,
our Lord Jesus Christ will come from heaven,
    bodily and visibly,
as he ascended,
    with great glory and majesty,
to declare himself the judge
    of the living and the dead.
He will burn this old world,
    in fire and flame,
    in order to cleanse it.

Then all human creatures will appear in person
before that great judge—
    men, women, and children,
    who have lived from the beginning until the end
    of the world.
They will be summoned there
by the voice of the archangel
and by the sound of the divine trumpet.[79]

---

*The Synod of 1985 directed that the following paragraph be taken from the body of the text and be placed in a footnote: And on this matter we denounce the Anabaptists, other anarchists,
and in general all those who want
to reject the authorities and civil officers
and to subvert justice
    by introducing common ownership of goods
    and corrupting the moral order
        that God has established among human beings.

For all those who died before that time
will be raised from the earth,
  their spirits being joined and united
  with their own bodies
  in which they lived.
And as for those who are still alive,
they will not die like the others
but will be changed "in the twinkling of an eye"
from "corruptible to incorruptible."[80]

Then "the books" (that is, the consciences) will be opened,
and the dead will be judged
  according to the things they did in the world,[81]
  whether good or evil.
Indeed, all people will give account
of all the idle words they have spoken,[82]
  which the world regards
  as only playing games.
And then the secrets and hypocrisies of men
will be publicly uncovered
in the sight of all.

Therefore,
with good reason
the thought of this judgment
is horrible and dreadful
to wicked and evil people.
But it is very pleasant
and a great comfort
to the righteous and elect,
  since their total redemption
  will then be accomplished.
They will then receive the fruits of their labor
  and of the trouble they have suffered;
their innocence will be openly recognized by all;
and they will see the terrible vengeance
  that God will bring on the evil ones
  who tyrannized, oppressed, and tormented them
    in this world.

The evil ones will be convicted
  by the witness of their own consciences,
and shall be made immortal—
  but only to be tormented
  in the everlasting fire
    prepared for the devil and his angels.[83]

In contrast,
the faithful and elect will be crowned
   with glory and honor.
The Son of God will "confess their names"[84]
   before God his Father and the holy and elect angels;
all tears will be "wiped from their eyes";[85]
and their cause—
   at present condemned as heretical and evil
   by many judges and civil officers—
will be acknowledged as the "cause of the Son of God."

And as a gracious reward
the Lord will make them possess a glory
such as the heart of man
could never imagine.

So we look forward to that great day with longing
in order to enjoy fully
the promises of God in Christ Jesus,
our Lord.

[79] 1 Thess. 4:16
[80] 1 Cor. 15:51–53
[81] Rev. 20:12
[82] Matt. 12:36
[83] Matt. 25:41
[84] Matt. 10:32
[85] Rev. 7:17